Set for the New York production of 'NIGHT MOTHER. Designed by Heidi Landesman.

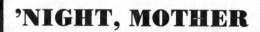

'NIGHT, MOTHER

By

MARSHA NORMAN

★

★

DRAMATISTS
PLAY SERVICE
INC.

'NIGHT, MOTHER
Copyright © 1983, Marsha Norman

'NIGHT, MOTHER opened on Broadway at the John Golden Theatre, on March 31, 1983, presented by Dann Byck, Wendell Cherry, The Shubert Organization and Frederick M. Zollo. The production was directed by Tom Moore, with sets and costumes by Heidi Landesman, and lights by James F. Ingalls. Steven Beckler was the production stage manager. The cast, in order of appearance, was as follows:

THELMA CATES .... Anne Pitoniak
JESSIE CATES........................... Kathy Bates

'NIGHT, MOTHER was originally produced by The American Repertory Theatre in Cambridge, Massachusetts in December, 1982.

'NIGHT, MOTHER was awarded the 1983 Pulitzer Prize for Drama.

CHARACTERS

JESSIE CATES — Jessie is in her late thirties or early forties, pale and vaguely unsteady, physically. It is only in the last year that Jessie has gained control of her mind and body, and tonight, she is determined to hold onto that control. She wears pants and a long black sweater with deep pockets one of which contains a notepad and there may be a pencil behind her ear or a pen clipped to one of the pockets of the sweater.

As a rule, Jessie doesn't feel much like talking. Other people have rarely found her quirky sense of humor amusing. She has a peaceful energy on this night, a sense of purpose, but is clearly aware of the time passing moment by moment. Oddly enough, Jessie has never been as communicative or as enjoyable as she is on this evening, but we must know she has not always been this way. There is a familiarity between these two women that comes from having lived together for a long time. There is a shorthand to the talk and a sense of routine comfort to the way they relate to each other physically. Naturally, there are also routine aggravations.

THELMA CATES — Thelma is Jessie's mother, in her late fifties or early sixties. She has begun to feel her age and so takes it easy when she can, or when it serves her purposes to let someone help her. But she speaks quickly and enjoys talking. She believes that things *are* what she says they are. Her sturdiness is more a mental quality than a physical one, finally. She is chatty and nosy and this is *her* house.

AUTHOR'S NOTE

The time is the present, with the action beginning about 8:15. Clocks onstage in the kitchen and on a table in the living room should run throughout the performance and be visible by the audience.

There will be no intermission.

The play takes place in a relatively new house built way out a country road, with a living room and connecting kitchen and a center hall that leads off to the bedrooms. A pull cord in the hall ceiling releases a ladder which leads to the attic. One of the bedrooms opens directly onto the hall and its entry should be visible by everyone in the audience. It should be, in fact, the focal point of the entire set and the lighting should make it disappear completely at times and draw the entire set into it at others. It is a point of both threat and promise. It is an ordinary door that opens onto absolute nothingness. That door is the point of all the action and the utmost care should be given its design and construction.

The living room is cluttered with magazines and needlework catalogues, ashtrays and candy dishes. Examples of Mama's needlework are everywhere—pillows, afghans and quilts, doilies and rugs, and they are quite nice examples. The house is more comfortable than messy, but there is quite a lot to keep in place here. It is more personal than charming. It is not quaint. Under no circumstances should the set and its dressing make a judgement about the intelligence or taste of Jessie and Thelma. It should simply indicate that they are very specific real people who happen to live in a particular part of the country. Heavy accents, which would further distance the audience from Jessie and Thelma are also wrong.

'NIGHT, MOTHER

Mama hums some odd little tune as she stretches to reach the cupcakes in a cabinet in the kitchen. She can't see them, but she can feel around for them, and she's eager to have one, so she's working pretty hard at it. This may be the most serious exercise Mama ever gets. She finds a cupcake, the coconut covered, raspberry and marshmallow filled kind known as a snowball, but sees that there's one missing from the package. She calls to Jessie, who is apparently somewhere else in the house.

MAMA. (*Unwrapping the cupcake.*) Jessie, it's the last snowball, sugar. Put it on the list, O.K.? And we're out of Hershey bars and where's that peanut brittle? I think maybe Dawson's been in it again. I ought to put a big mirror on the refrigerator door. That'll keep him out of my treats, won't it? You hear me, honey? (*Then more to herself.*) I hate it when the coconut falls off. Why does the coconut fall off? (*Jessie enters from her bedroom, carrying a stack of newspapers.*)
JESSIE. We got any old towels?
MAMA. There you are!
JESSIE. (*Holding a towel that was on the stack of newspapers.*) Towels you don't want any more. (*And picking up Mama's snowball wrapper.*) How about this swimming towel

9

Loretta gave us? Beach towel, that's the name of it. You want it? (*Mama shakes her head No.*)

MAMA. What have you been doing in there?

JESSIE. And a big piece of plastic like a rubber sheet or something. Garbage bags would do if there's enough.

MAMA. Don't go making a big mess, Jessie. It's eight o'clock already.

JESSIE. Maybe an old blanket or towels we got in a soap box sometime?

MAMA. I said don't make a mess. Your hair is black enough, hon.

JESSIE. (*Continues to search the kitchen cabinets, finding two or three more towels to add to her stack.*) It's not for my hair, Mama. What about some old pillows anywhere or a foam cushion out of a yard chair would be real good.

MAMA. You haven't forgot what night it is, have you? (*Holding up her fingernails.*) They're all chipped, see? I've been waiting all week, Jess. It's Saturday night, sugar.

JESSIE. I know. I got it on the schedule.

MAMA. (*Crossing to the living room.*) You want me to wash 'em now or are you making your mess first? (*Looking at the snowball.*) We're out of these. Did I say that already?

JESSIE. There's more coming tomorrow. I ordered you a whole case.

MAMA. (*Checking the TV Guide.*) A whole case will go stale, Jessie.

JESSIE. They can go in the freezer til you're ready for them. Where's Daddy's gun?

MAMA. In the attic.

JESSIE. Where in the attic? I looked your whole nap and couldn't find it anywhere.

MAMA. One of his shoeboxes, I think.

JESSIE. Full of shoes. I looked already.

MAMA. Well, you didn't look good enough, then. There's that box from the ones he wore to the hospital. When he

10

died, they told me I could have them back, but I never did like those shoes.

JESSIE. (*Pulling them out of her pocket.*) I found the bullets. They were in an old milkcan.

MAMA. (*As Jessie starts for the hall.*) Dawson took the shotgun, didn't he? Hand me that basket, hon.

JESSIE. (*Gets the basket for her.*) Dawson better not've taken that pistol.

MAMA. (*Stopping her again.*) Now my glasses, please. (*Jessie returns to get the glasses.*) I told him to take those rubber boots too, but he said they were for fishing. I told him to take up fishing. (*Jessie reaches for the cleaning spray, and cleans Mama's glasses for her.*)

JESSIE. He's just too lazy to climb up there, Mama. Or maybe he's just being smart. That floor's not very steady.

MAMA. (*Getting out a piece of knitting.*) It's not a floor at all, hon, it's a board now and then. Measure this for me. I need six inches.

JESSIE. (*As she measures.*) Dawson could probably use some of those clothes up there. Somebody should have them. You ought to call the Salvation Army before the whole thing falls in on you. Six inches exactly.

MAMA. It's plenty safe! As long as you don't go up there.

JESSIE. (*Turning to go again.*) I'm careful.

MAMA. What do you want the gun for, Jess?

JESSIE. (*Not returning this time. Opening the ladder in the hall.*) Protection. (*She steadies the ladder as Mama talks.*)

MAMA. You take the TV way too serious, hon. I've never seen a criminal in my life. This is way too far to come for what's out here to steal. Never seen a one.

JESSIE. (*Taking her first step up.*) Except for Ricky.

MAMA. Ricky is mixed up. That's not a crime.

JESSIE. Get your hands washed. I'll be right back. And get 'em real dry. You dry your hands til I get back or it's no go, all right?

11

MAMA. I thought Dawson told you not to go up those stairs.

JESSIE. (*Going up.*) He did.

MAMA. I don't like the idea of a gun, Jess.

JESSIE. (*Calling down from the attic.*) Which shoebox, do you remember?

MAMA. Black.

JESSIE. The box was black?

MAMA. The shoes were black.

JESSIE. That doesn't help much, Mother.

MAMA. I'm not trying to help, sugar. (*No answer.*) We don't have anything anybody'd want, Jessie. I mean, I don't even want what we got, Jessie.

JESSIE. Neither do I. Wash your hands. (*Mama gets up now and crosses to stand under the ladder.*)

MAMA. You come down from there before you have a fit. I can't come up and get you, you know.

JESSIE. I know.

MAMA. We'll just hand it over to 'em when they come, how's that? Whatever they want, the criminals.

JESSIE. That's a good idea, Mama.

MAMA. Ricky will grow out of this and be a real fine boy, Jess. But I have to tell you, I wouldn't want Ricky to know we had a gun in the house.

JESSIE. Here it is. I found it.

MAMA. It's just something Ricky's going through. Maybe he's in with some bad people. He just needs some time, sugar. He'll get back in school or get a job or one day you'll get a call and he'll say he's sorry for all the trouble he's caused and invite you out for supper someplace dressup.

JESSIE. (*Coming back down the stairs now.*) Don't worry. It's not for him, it's for me.

MAMA. I didn't think you would shoot your own boy, Jessie. I know you've felt like it, well, we've all felt like shooting somebody, but we don't do it. I just don't think we need . . .

12

JESSIE. (*Interrupting.*) Your hands aren't washed. Do you want a manicure or not?

MAMA. Yes I do, but . . .

JESSIE. (*Crossing to the chair.*) Then wash your hands and don't talk to me any more about Ricky. Those two rings he took were the last valuable things *I* had so now he's started in on other people, door to door. I hope they put him away sometime. I'd turn him in, myself, if I knew where he was.

MAMA. You don't mean that.

JESSIE. Every word. Wash your hands and that's the last time I'm telling you. (*Jessie sits down with the gun and starts cleaning it, pushing the cylinder out, checking to see that the chambers and barrel are empty, then putting some oil on a small patch of cloth and pushing it through the barrel with the push rod that was in the box. Mama goes to the kitchen and washes her hands, as instructed, trying not to show her concern about the gun.*)

MAMA. I shoulda got you to bring down that milk can. Agnes Fletcher sold hers to somebody with a flea market for forty dollars apiece.

JESSIE. I'll go back and get it in a minute. There's a wagon wheel up there too. There's even a churn. I'll get it all if you want.

MAMA. (*Coming over now, taking over now.*) What are you doing?

JESSIE. The barrel has to be clean, Mama. Old powder, dust gets in it . . .

MAMA. What for?

JESSIE. I told you.

MAMA. (*Reaching for the gun.*) And I told you, we don't get criminals out here.

JESSIE. (*Quickly pulling it to her.*) And I told you . . . (*Then trying to be calm.*) The gun is for me.

MAMA. Well you can have it if you want. When I die, you'll get it all anyway.

JESSIE. I'm going to kill myself, Mama.

13

MAMA. (*Returning to the sofa.*) Very funny. Very funny.

JESSIE. I am.

MAMA. (*Quickly, irritated.*) You are not! Don't even say such a thing, Jessie.

JESSIE. How would you know if I didn't say it? You want it to be a surprise? You're lying there in your bed or maybe you're just brushing your teeth and you hear this . . . noise down the hall?

MAMA. Kill yourself.

JESSIE. Shoot myself. In a couple of hours.

MAMA. It must be time for your medicine.

JESSIE. Took it already.

MAMA. Then what's the matter with you?

JESSIE. Not a thing. Feel fine.

MAMA. You feel fine. You're just going to kill yourself.

JESSIE. Waited until I felt good enough, in fact.

MAMA. Don't make jokes, Jessie. I'm too old for jokes.

JESSIE. It's not a joke, Mama. (*Mama watches for a moment in silence.*)

MAMA. That gun's no good, you know. He broke it right before he died. He dropped it in the mud one day.

JESSIE. Seems O.K. (*Jessie spins the chamber, cocks the pistol and pulls the trigger. The gun is not yet loaded, so all we hear is the click, but it will definitely work. It's also obvious that Jessie knows her way around a gun. Mama cannot speak.*) I had Cecil's all ready in there, just in case I couldn't find this one, but I'd rather use Daddy's.

MAMA. Those bullets are at least 15 years old.

JESSIE. (*Pulls out another box.*) These are from last week.

MAMA. Where did you get those?

JESSIE. Feed store Dawson told me about.

MAMA. Dawson!

JESSIE. I told him I was worried about prowlers. He said he thought it was a good idea. He told me what kind to ask for.

MAMA. If he had any idea . . .

JESSIE. He took it as a compliment. He thought I might be

14

taking an interest in things. He got through telling me all about the bullets and then he said we ought to talk like this more often.

MAMA. And where was I while this was going on?

JESSIE. On the phone with Agnes. About the milk can, I guess. Anyway, I asked Dawson if he thought they'd send me some bullets and he said he's just call for me, because he *knew* they'd send them if he told them to. And he was absolutely right. Here they are.

MAMA. How could he do that?

JESSIE. Just trying to help, Mama.

MAMA. And then I told you where the gun was.

JESSIE. (*Smiling, enjoying this joke.*) See? Everybody's doing what they can.

MAMA. You told me it was for protection!

JESSIE. It *is*! I'm still doing your nails, though. Want to try that new Chinaberry color?

MAMA. Well, I'm calling Dawson right now. We'll just see what he has to say about this little stunt.

JESSIE. Dawson doesn't have any more to do with this.

MAMA. He's your brother.

JESSIE. And that's all.

MAMA. (*Stands up, moves toward the phone.*) Dawson will put a stop to this. Yes he will. He'll take the gun away.

JESSIE. If you call him, I'll just have to do it before he gets here. Soon as you hang up the phone, I'll just walk in the bedroom and lock the door.

MAMA. You will not! This is crazy talk, Jessie!

JESSIE. Dawson will get here just in time to help you clean up. Go ahead, call him. Then call the police. Then call the funeral home. Then call Loretta and see if *she'll* do your nails. (*Mama goes directly to the telephone and starts to dial, but Jessie is fast, coming up behind her and taking the receiver out of her hand, putting it back down. Jessie, firm and quiet.*) I said No. This is private. Dawson is not invited.

MAMA. Just me.

JESSIE. I don't want anybody else over here. Just you and me. If Dawson comes over it'll make me feel stupid for not doing it ten years ago.

MAMA. I think we better call the doctor. Or how about the ambulance. You like that one driver, I know. What's his name, Timmy? Get you somebody to talk to.

JESSIE. (*Going back to her chair.*) I'm through talking, Mama. You're it. No more.

MAMA. We're just going to sit around like every other night in the world and then you're going to kill yourself? (*Jessie doesn't answer.*) You'll miss. (*Again, there is no response.*) You'll just wind up a vegetable. How would you like that? Shoot your ear off? You know what the doctor said about getting excited. You'll cock the pistol and have a fit.

JESSIE. I think I can kill myself, Mama.

MAMA. You're not going to kill yourself, Jessie. You're not even upset! (*And Jessie smiles, or laughs quietly, and Mama tries a different approach.*) People don't really kill themselves, Jessie. No, Mam, doesn't make sense, unless you're retarded or deranged and you're as normal as they come, Jessie, for the most part. We're all *afraid* to die.

JESSIE. I'm not, Mama. I'm cold all the time anyway.

MAMA. That's ridiculous.

JESSIE. It's exactly what I want. It's dark and quiet.

MAMA. So is the back yard, Jessie! Close your eyes. Stuff cotton in your ears. Take a nap! It's quiet in your room. I'll leave the TV off all night.

JESSIE. So quiet I don't know it's quiet. So nobody can get me.

MAMA. You don't know what dead is like. It might not be quiet at all. What if it's like an alarm clock and you can't wake up so you can't shut it off. Ever.

JESSIE. Dead is everybody and everything I ever knew, gone. Dead is dead quiet.

MAMA. It's a sin. You'll go to hell.

JESSIE. Uh-huh.

MAMA. You will!

JESSIE. Jesus was a suicide, if you ask me.

MAMA. You'll go to hell just for saying that. Jessie!

JESSIE. (*Genuine surprise.*) I didn't know I thought that.

MAMA. Jessie! (*Jessie doesn't answer. She puts the now loaded gun back in the box and crosses to the kitchen. But Mama is afraid she is headed for the bedroom. Mama, in panic.*) You can't use my towels! They're my towels. I've had them for a long time. I like my towels.

JESSIE. I asked you if you wanted that swimming towel and you said you didn't.

MAMA. And you can't use your father's gun either. It's mine now too. And you can't do it in my house.

JESSIE. Oh come on.

MAMA. No. You can't do it. I won't let you. The house is in my name.

JESSIE. I have to go in the bedroom and lock the door behind me so they won't arrest you for killing me. They'll probably test your hands for gunpowder anyway, but you'll pass.

MAMA. Not in my house!

JESSIE. If I'd known you were going to act like this, I wouldn't have told you.

MAMA. How am I supposed to act? Tell you to go ahead? O.K. by me, sugar. Might try it myself. What took you so long?

JESSIE. There's just no point in fighting me over it, that's all. Want some coffee?

MAMA. Your birthday's coming up, Jessie. Don't you want to know what we got you?

JESSIE. You got me dusting powder, Loretta got me a new housecoat, pink probably and Dawson got me new slippers, too small, but they go with the robe, he'll say. (*Mama cannot speak.*) Right? (*Apparently Jessie is right.*) Be back in a minute. (*Jessie takes the gun box, puts it on top of the stack of towels and garbage bags and takes them into her bedroom.*

17

Mama, alone for a moment, goes to the phone, picks up the receiver, looks toward the bedroom, starts to dial and then replaces the receiver in its cradle as Jessie walks back into the room. Jessie wonders, silently. They have lived together for so long, there is very rarely any reason for one to ask what the other was about to do.)

MAMA. I started to, but I didn't. I didn't call him.

JESSIE. Good. Thank you.

MAMA. (*Starting over, a new approach.*) What's this all about, Jessie?

JESSIE. About? (*Jessie now begins the next task she had "on the schedule," which is refilling all the candy jars, taking the empty papers out of the boxes of chocolates, etc. Mama generally snitches when Jessie does this. Not tonight, though. Nevertheless, Jessie offers.*)

MAMA. What did I do?

JESSIE. Nothing. Want a caramel?

MAMA. (*Ignoring the candy.*) You're mad at me.

JESSIE. Not a bit. I am worried about you, but I'm going to do what I can before I go. We're not just going to sit around tonight. I made a list of things.

MAMA. What things?

JESSIE. How the washer works. Things like that.

MAMA. Did you grow up wearing dirty clothes?

JESSIE. No.

MAMA. I know how the washer works. You put the clothes in. You put the soap in. You turn it on. You wait.

JESSIE. You do something else. You don't just wait.

MAMA. Whatever else you find to do you're still mainly waiting. The waiting's the worst part of it. The waiting's what you pay somebody else to do, if you can.

JESSIE. (*Nodding.*) O.K. Where do we keep the soap?

MAMA. I could find it.

JESSIE. See?

MAMA. If you're mad about doing the wash, we can get Loretta to do it.

18

JESSIE. Oh now, that might be worth staying to see.

MAMA. She'd never in her life, would she?

JESSIE. Nope.

MAMA. What's the matter with her?

JESSIE. She thinks she's better than we are. She's not.

MAMA. Maybe if she didn't wear that yellow all the time.

JESSIE. The washer repair number is on a little card taped to the side of the machine.

MAMA. Loretta doesn't ever have to come over here again. Dawson can just leave her at home when he comes. And we won't ever see Dawson either if he bothers you. Does he bother you?

JESSIE. Sure he does. Be sure you clean out the lint tray every time you use the dryer. But don't ever put your house shoes in, it'll melt the soles.

MAMA. What does Dawson do, that bothers you?

JESSIE. He just calls me Jess like he knows who he's talking to. He's always wondering what I do all day. I mean, I wonder that myself, but it's my day, so it's mine to wonder about, not his.

MAMA. Family is just accident, Jessie. It's nothing personal, hon. They don't mean to get on your nerves. They don't even mean to be your family, they just are.

JESSIE. They know too much.

MAMA. About what?

JESSIE. They know things about you, and they learned it before you had a chance to say whether you wanted them to know it or not. They were there when it happened and it don't belong to them, it belongs to you, only they got it. Like my mail order bra got delivered to their house.

MAMA. By accident!

JESSIE. All the same . . . they opened it. They saw the little rosebuds on it. (*Offering her another candy.*) Chewy mint?

MAMA. (*Shaking her head no.*) What do they know about you? I'll tell them never to talk about it again. Is it Ricky or Cecil or your fits or your hair is falling out or you drink too

19

much coffee or you never go out of the house or what?

JESSIE. I just don't like their talk. The account at the grocery is in Dawson's name when you call. The number's on a whole list of numbers on the back cover of the phone book.

MAMA. Well! Now we're getting somewhere. They're none of them ever setting foot in this house again.

JESSIE. It's not them, Mother. I wouldn't kill myself just to get away from them.

MAMA. You leave the room when they come over, anyway.

JESSIE. I stay as long as I can. Besides, it's you they come to see.

MAMA. That's because I stay in the room when they come.

JESSIE. It's not them.

MAMA. Then what is it?

JESSIE. (*Checking the list on her notepad.*) The grocery won't deliver on Saturday any more. And if you want your order the same day, you have to call before 10. And they won't deliver less than 15 dollars worth. What I do is tell them what we need and tell them to add on cigarettes until it gets to 15 dollars.

MAMA. It's Ricky. You're trying to get through to him.

JESSIE. If I thought I could do that, I would stay.

MAMA. Make him sorry he hurt you, then. That's it, isn't it?

JESSIE. He's hurt me, I've hurt him. We're about even.

MAMA. You'll be telling him killing is O.K. with you, you know. Want him to start killing next? Nothing wrong with it. Mom did it.

JESSIE. Only a matter of time anyway, Mama. When the call comes, you let Dawson handle it.

MAMA. Honey, nothing says those calls are always going to be some new trouble he's into. You could get one that he's got a job, that he's getting married, or how about he's joined the army, wouldn't that be nice?

JESSIE. If you call The Sweet Tooth before you call the grocery, that Susie will take your fudge next door to the grocery and it'll all come out together. Be sure you talk to

Susie, though. She won't let them put it in the bottom of a sack like that one time, remember?

MAMA. Ricky could come over, you know. What if he calls us?

JESSIE. It's not Ricky, Mama.

MAMA. Or anybody could call us, Jessie.

JESSIE. Not on Saturday night, Mama.

MAMA. Then what is it? Are you sick? If your gums are swelling again, we can get you to the dentist in the morning.

JESSIE. No. Can you order your medicine or do you want Dawson to? I've got a note to him. I'll add that to it if you want.

MAMA. Your eyes don't look right. I thought so yesterday.

JESSIE. That was just the ragweed. I'm not sick.

MAMA. Epilepsy is sick, Jessie.

JESSIE. It won't kill me. (*A pause.*) If it would, I wouldn't have to.

MAMA. You don't *have* to.

JESSIE. No, I don't. That's what I like about it.

MAMA. Well I won't let you!

JESSIE. It's not up to you.

MAMA. Jessie!

JESSIE. I want to hang a big sign around my neck, like Daddy's on the barn. Gone Fishing.

MAMA. You don't like it here.

JESSIE. (*Smiles.*) Exactly.

MAMA. I meant here in my house.

JESSIE. I know you did.

MAMA. You never should have moved back in here with me. If you'd kept your little house or found another place when Cecil left you, you'd have made some new friends at least. Had a life to lead. Had your own things around you. Give Ricky a place to come see you. You never should've come here.

JESSIE. Maybe.

MAMA. But I didn't force you, did I?

JESSIE. If it was a mistake, we made it together. You took me in. I appreciate that.

MAMA. You didn't have any business being by yourself right then, but I can see how you might want a place of your own. You could be as close or as far away as you wanted. A grown woman should . . .

JESSIE. Mama . . . I'm just not having a very good time and I don't have any reason to think it'll get anything but worse. I'm tired. I'm hurt. I'm sad. I feel used.

MAMA. Tired of what?

JESSIE. It all.

MAMA. What does that mean?

JESSIE. I can't say it any better.

MAMA. Well, you'll have to say it better because I'm not letting you alone til you do. What were those other things. Hurt . . . (*Before Jessie can answer.*) You had this all ready to say to me, didn't you? Did you write this down? How long have you been thinking about this?

JESSIE. Off and on, ten years. On all the time, since Christmas.

MAMA. What happened at Christmas?

JESSIE. Nothing.

MAMA. So why Christmas?

JESSIE. That's it. On the nose. (*A pause. Mama knows exactly what Jessie means. She was there, too, after all. Jessie, putting the candy sacks away.*) See where all this is? Red hots up front, sour balls and horehound mixed together in this one sack. New packages of toffee and licorice right in back there.

MAMA. Go back to your list. You're hurt by what?

JESSIE. (*Mama knows perfectly well.*) Mama . . .

MAMA. O.K. Sad about what? There's nothing real sad going on right now. If it was after your divorce or something, that would make sense.

JESSIE. (*Looks at her list, then opens the drawer.*) Now, this drawer has everything in it that there's no better place for. Extension cords, batteries for the radio, extra lighters, sand paper, masking tape, Elmer's glue, thumbtacks, that kind of stuff. The mousetraps are under the sink, but you call Dawson if you've got one and let him do it.

MAMA. Sad about what?

JESSIE. The way things are.

MAMA. Not good enough. What things?

JESSIE. Oh, everything from you and me to Red China.

MAMA. I think we can leave the Chinese out of this.

JESSIE. (*Crosses back into the living room.*) There's extra lightbulbs in a box in the hall closet. And we've got a couple of packages of fuses in the fuse box. There's candles and matches in the top of the broom closet, but if the lights go out, just call Dawson and sit tight. But don't open the refrigerator door. Things will stay cool in there as long as you keep the door shut.

MAMA. I asked you a question.

JESSIE. I read the paper. I don't like how things are. And they're not any better out there than they are in here.

MAMA. If you're doing this because of the newspapers, I can sure fix that!

JESSIE. There's just more of it on TV.

MAMA. (*Kicks the television.*) Take it out then!

JESSIE. You wouldn't do that.

MAMA. Watch me.

JESSIE. What would you do all day?

MAMA. (*Desperate.*) Sing. (*Jessie laughs.*) I would too. You want to watch? I'll sing til morning to keep you alive, Jessie, please!

JESSIE. No. (*Then affectionately.*) It's a funny idea, though. What do you sing?

MAMA. (*Has no idea how to answer this.*) We've got a good life here!

JESSIE. (*Going back into the kitchen.*) I called this morning and cancelled the papers, except for Sunday, for your puzzles, you'll still get that one.

MAMA. Let's get another dog, Jessie! You liked a big dog,

didn't you, that King dog, didn't you?

JESSIE. (*Washing her hands.*) I did like that King dog, yes.

MAMA. I'm so dumb. He's the one run under the tractor.

JESSIE. That makes him dumb, not you.

MAMA. For bringing it up.

JESSIE. It's O.K. Handi-wipes and sponges under the sink.

MAMA. We could get a new dog and keep him in the house. Dogs are cheap!

JESSIE. (*Now getting big pill jars out of the cabinet.*) No.

MAMA. Something for you to take care of.

JESSIE. I've had you, Mama.

MAMA. (*Frantically starts filling pill bottles.*) You do too much for me. I can fill pill bottles all day, Jessie, and change the shelf-paper and wash the floor when I get through. You just watch me. You don't have to do another thing in this house if you don't want to. You don't have to take care of me, Jessie.

JESSIE. I know that. You've just been letting me do it so I'll have something to do, haven't you?

MAMA. (*Realizing this was a mistake.*) I don't do it as well as you, I just meant if it tires you out or makes you feel used . . .

JESSIE. Mama, I know you used to ride the bus. Riding the bus and it's hot and bumpy and crowded and too noisy and more than anything in the world you want to get off and the only reason in the world you don't get off is it's still 50 blocks from where you're going? Well, I can get off right now if I want to, because even if I ride 50 more years and get off then, it's the same place when I step down to it. Whenever I feel like it, I can get off. As soon as I've had enough, it's my stop. I've had enough.

MAMA. You're feeling sorry for yourself!

JESSIE. The plumber's helper is under the sink, too.

MAMA. You're not having a good time! Whoever promised you a good time? Do you think I've had a good time?

24

JESSIE. I think you're pretty happy, yeah. You have things you like to do.

MAMA. Like what?

JESSIE. Like crochet.

MAMA. I'll teach you to crochet.

JESSIE. I can't do any of that nice work, Mama.

MAMA. Good time don't come looking for you, Jessie. You could work some puzzles or put in a garden or go to the store. Let's call a taxi and go to the A & P.

JESSIE. I shopped you up for about two weeks already. You're not going to need toilet paper til Thanksgiving.

MAMA. (*Interrupting.*) You're acting like some little brat, Jessie. You're mad and everybody's boring and you don't have anything to do and you don't like me and you don't like going out and you don't like staying in and you never talk on the phone and you don't watch TV and you're miserable and it's your own sweet fault.

JESSIE. And it's time I did something about it.

MAMA. Not something like killing yourself. Something like . . . buying us all new dishes! I'd like that. Or maybe the doctor would let you get a driver's license now, or I know what let's do right this minute, let's rearrange the furniture.

JESSIE. I'll do that. If you want. I always thought if the TV was somewhere else, you wouldn't get such a glare on it during the day. I'll do whatever you want before I go.

MAMA. (*Badly frightened by those words.*) You could get a job!

JESSIE. I took that telephone sales job and I didn't even make enough money to pay the phone bill, and I tried to work at the gift shop at the hospital and they said I made people real uncomfortable smiling at them the way I did.

MAMA. You could keep books. You kept your Dad's books.

JESSIE. But nobody ever checked them.

MAMA. When he died, they checked them.

25

JESSIE. And that's when they took the books away from me.

MAMA. That's because without him there wasn't any business, Jessie!

JESSIE (*Puts the pill bottles away now.*) You know I couldn't work. I can't do anything. I've never been around people my whole life except when I went to the hospital. I could have a seizure any time. What good would a job do? The kind of job I could get would make me feel worse.

MAMA. Jessie!

JESSIE. It's true!

MAMA. It's what you think is true!

JESSIE. (*Struck by the clarity of that.*) That's right. It's what I think is true.

MAMA. (*Hysterical.*) But I can't do anything about that!

JESSIE. (*Quietly.*) No. You can't. (*Mama slumps, if not physically, at least emotionally.*) And I can't do anything either, about my life, to change it, make it better, make me feel better about it. Like it better, make it work. But I can stop it. Shut it down, turn it off like the radio when there's nothing on I want to listen to. It's all I really have that belongs to me and I'm going to say what happens to it. And it's going to stop. And I'm going to stop it. So. Let's just have a good time.

MAMA. Have a good time.

JESSIE. We can't go on fussing all night. I mean, I could ask you things I always wanted to know and you could make me some hot chocolate. The old way.

MAMA. (*In despair.*) It takes cocoa, Jessie.

JESSIE. (*Gets it out of the cabinet.*) I bought cocoa, Mama. And I'd like to have a caramel apple and do your nails.

MAMA. You didn't eat a bite of supper.

JESSIE. Does that mean I can't have a caramel apple?

MAMA. Of course not. I mean, (*Smiling a little.*) of course you can have a caramel apple.

JESSIE. I thought I could.

MAMA. I make the best caramel apples in the world.

26

JESSIE. I know you do.

MAMA. Or used to. And you don't get cocoa like mine anywhere any more.

JESSIE. It takes time, I know, but . . .

MAMA. The salt is the trick.

JESSIE. Trouble and everything.

MAMA. (*Backing away toward the stove.*) It's no trouble. What trouble? You put it in the pan and stir it up. All right. Fine. Caramel apples. Cocoa. O.K. (*Jessie walks to the counter to retrieve her cigarettes as Mama looks for the right pan. There are brief near smiles and maybe Mama clears her throat. We have a truce, for the moment. A genuine, but nevertheless uneasy one. Jessie, who has been in constant motion since the beginning, now seems content to sit. Mama starts looking for a pan to make the cocoa, getting out all the pans in the cabinets in the process. It looks like she's making a mess on purpose so Jessie will have to put them all away again. Mama is buying time, or trying to, and entertaining.*)

JESSIE. You talk to Agnes today?

MAMA. She's calling me from a pay phone this week. God only knows why. She has a perfectly good trimline at home.

JESSIE. (*Laughing.*) Well, how is she?

MAMA. How is she every day, Jessie? Nuts.

JESSIE. Is she really crazy or just silly?

MAMA. No, she's really crazy. She was probably using the pay phone because she had another little fire problem at home.

JESSIE. Mother . . .

MAMA. I'm serious! Agnes Fletcher's burned down every house she ever lived in. Eight fires and she's due for a new one any day now.

JESSIE. (*Laughing.*) No!

MAMA. (*Really enjoying herself now.*) Wouldn't surprise me a bit.

JESSIE. (*Laughing.*) Why didn't you tell me this before? Why isn't she locked up somewhere?

27

MAMA. Cause nobody ever got hurt, I guess. Agnes woke everybody up to watch the fires as soon as she set 'em.

JESSIE. That's thoughtful, I guess.

MAMA. One time she set out porch chairs and served lemondade.

JESSIE. (*Shaking her head.*) Real lemondade?

MAMA. The houses they lived in, you knew they were going to fall down anyway, so why wait for it, is all I could ever make out about it. Agnes likes a feeling of accomplishment.

JESSIE. (*Thinks about that a minute.*) Good for her.

MAMA. (*Finding the pan she wants.*) Why are you asking about Agnes? One cup or two?

JESSIE. One. She's your friend. No marshmallows.

MAMA. (*Getting the milk, etc.*) You have to have marshmallows. That's the old way, Jess. Two or three? Three is better.

JESSIE. Three then. Her whole house burns up? Her clothes and pillows and everything? I'm not sure I believe this.

MAMA. When she was a girl, Jess, not now. Long time ago. But she's still got it in her, I'm sure of it.

JESSIE. She wouldn't burn her house down now. Where would she go? She can't get Buster to build her a new one, he's dead. How could she burn it up?

MAMA. Be exciting though if she did. You never know.

JESSIE. You do too know, Mama. She wouldn't do it.

MAMA. (*Forced to admit, but reluctant.*) I guess not.

JESSIE. What else? Why does she wear all those whistles around her neck?

MAMA. Why does she have a house full of birds?

JESSIE. I didn't know she had a house full of birds!

MAMA. Well, she does. And she says they just follow her home. Well, I know for a fact she's still paying on the last parrot she bought. You gotta keep your life filled up, she says. She says a lot of stupid things. (*Jessie laughs, Mama continues, convinced she's getting somewhere.*) It's all that okra she eats. You can't just willy-nilly eat okra two meals a day and expect to get away with it. Made her crazy.

JESSIE. She really eats okra twice a day? Where does she get it in the winter?

MAMA. Well, she eats it a lot. Maybe not two meals, but . . .

JESSIE. More than the average person.

MAMA. (*Beginning to get irritated.*) I don't know how much okra the average person eats.

JESSIE. Do you know how much okra Agnes eats?

MAMA. No.

JESSIE. How many birds does she have?

MAMA. Two.

JESSIE. Then what are the whistles for?

MAMA. They're not real whistles. Just little plastic ones on a necklace she won playing bingo and I only told you about it because I thought I might get a laugh out of you for once even if it wasn't the truth, Jessie. Things don't have to be true to talk about 'em, you know.

JESSIE. Why won't she come over here? (*Mama is suddenly quiet, but the cocoa and milk are in the pan now, so she lights the stove and starts stirring.*)

MAMA. Well, now, what a good idea. We should've had more cocoa. Cocoa is perfect.

JESSIE. Except you don't like milk.

MAMA. (*Another attempt, but not as energetic.*) I hate milk. Coats your throat as bad as okra. Something just downright disgusting about it.

JESSIE. It's because of me, isn't it?

MAMA. No, Jess.

JESSIE. Yes, Mama.

MAMA. O.K. Yes, then, but she's crazy. She's as crazy as they come. She's a lunatic.

JESSIE. What is it exactly? Did I say something, sometime? Or did she see me have a fit and's afraid I might have another one if she came over or what?

MAMA. I guess.

29

JESSIE. You guess what? What's she ever said? She must've given you some reason.

MAMA. Your hands are cold.

JESSIE. What difference does that make?

MAMA. Like a corpse, she says, and I'm gonna be one soon enough as it is.

JESSIE. That's crazy.

MAMA. That's Agnes. "Jessie's shook the hand of death and I can't take the chance it's catching, Thelma, so I ain't comin' over and you can understand or not, but I ain't comin. I'll come up the driveway, but that's as far as I go."

JESSIE. (*Laughing, relieved.*) I thought she didn't like me! She's scared of me! How about that! Scared of me.

MAMA. I could make her come over here, Jessie. I could call her up right now and she could bring the birds and come visit. I didn't know you ever thought about her at all. I'll tell her she just has to come and she'll come all right. She owes me one.

JESSIE. No, that's all right. I just wondered about it. When I'm in the hospital, does she come over here?

MAMA. Her kitchen is just a tiny thing. When she comes over here, she feels like . . . (*Toning it down a little.*) Well, we all like a change of scene, don't we?

JESSIE. (*Playing along.*) Sure we do. Plus there's no birds diving around.

MAMA. I hate those birds. She says I don't understand them. What's there to understand about birds?

JESSIE. Why Agnes likes them, for one thing. Why they stay with her when they could be outside with the other birds. How much water they need. What their singing means. How they fly. What they think Agnes is.

MAMA. Why do you have to know so much about things, Jessie? There's just not that much *to* things that I could ever see.

JESSIE. That you could ever *tell*, you mean. You didn't have to lie to me about Agnes.

30

MAMA. I didn't lie. You never asked before!

JESSIE. You lied about setting fire to all those houses and about how many birds she has and how much okra she eats and why she won't come over here. If I have to keep dragging the truth out of you, this is going to take all night.

MAMA. That's fine with me. I'm not a bit sleepy.

JESSIE. Mama . . .

MAMA. All right. Ask me whatever you want. Here. (*And they come to an awkward stop, as the cocoa is ready and Mama pours it into the cups Jessie has ready.*)

JESSIE. (*As Mama takes her first sip.*) Did you love Daddy?

MAMA. No.

JESSIE. (*Pleased that Mama understands the rules better now.*) I didn't think so. Were you really fifteen when you married him?

MAMA. The way he told it? I'm sitting in the mud, he comes along, drags me in the kitchen, "She's been there ever since?"

JESSIE. Yes.

MAMA. No. It was a big fat lie, the whole thing. He just thought it was funnier that way. God, this milk in here.

JESSIE. The cocoa helps.

MAMA. (*Pleased that they agree on this, at least.*) Not enough, though, does it? You can still taste it, can't you?

JESSIE. Yeah, it's pretty bad. I thought it was my memory that was bad, but it's not. It's the milk, all right.

MAMA. It's a real waste of chocolate. You don't have to finish it.

JESSIE. (*Puts her cup down.*) Thanks though.

MAMA. I should've known not to make it. I knew you wouldn't like it. You never did like it.

JESSIE. You didn't ever love him or he did something and you stopped loving him or what?

MAMA. He felt sorry for me. He wanted a plain country woman and that's what he married and then he held it against me the rest of my life like I was supposed to change

31

and surprise him somehow. Like I remember this one day he was standing on the porch and I told him to get a shirt on and he went in and got one and then he said, real peaceful, but to the point, "You're right, Thelma. If God had meant for people to go around without any clothes on, they'd have been born that way."

JESSIE. (*Sees Mama's hurt.*) He didn't mean anything by that, Mama.

MAMA. He never said a word he didn't have to, Jessie. That was probably all he'd said to me all day, Jessie. So if he said it, there was something to it, but I never did figure that one out. What did that mean?

JESSIE. I don't know. I liked him better than you did, but I didn't know him any better.

MAMA. How could I love him, Jessie. I didn't have a thing he wanted. (*Jessie doesn't answer.*) He got his share, though. You loved him enough for both of us. You followed him around like some . . . Jessie, all the man ever did was farm and sit . . . and try to think of somebody to sell the farm to.

JESSIE. Or make me a boyfriend out of pipe cleaners and sit back and smile like the stick man was about to dance and wasn't I going to get a kick out of that. Or sit up with a sick cow all night and leave me a chain of sleepy stick elephants on my bed in the morning.

MAMA. Or just sit.

JESSIE. I liked him sitting. Big old faded blue man in the chair. Quiet.

MAMA. Agnes gets more talk out of her birds than I got from the two of you. He could've had that Gone Fishing sign around his neck in that chair. I saw him stare off at the water. I saw him look at the weather rolling in. I got where I could practically see the boat myself. But you, you knew what he was thinking about and you're going to tell me.

JESSIE. I don't know, Mama! His life, I guess. His corn. His boots. Us. Things. You know.

MAMA. No I don't know, Jessie! You had those quiet little

conversations after supper every night. What were you whispering about?

JESSIE. We weren't whispering, you were just across the room.

MAMA. What did you talk about?

JESSIE. We talked about why black socks are warmer than blue socks. Is that something to go tell Mother? You were just jealous because I'd rather talk to him than wash the dishes with you.

MAMA. I was jealous because you'd rather talk to him than anything! (*Jessie reaches across the table for the small clock and starts to wind it.*) If I had died instead of him, he wouldn't have taken you in like I did.

JESSIE. I wouldn't have expected him to.

MAMA. Then what would you have done?

JESSIE. Come visit.

MAMA. Oh I see. He died and left you stuck with me and you're mad about it.

JESSIE. (*Getting up from the table.*) Not any more. He didn't mean to. I didn't have to come here. We've been through this.

MAMA. Or maybe you think if I'd loved him more, or at all, he'd still be alive.

JESSIE. I never thought that.

MAMA. He felt sorry for you, too, Jessie, don't kid yourself about that. He said you were a runt and he said it from the day you were born and he said you didn't have a chance.

JESSIE. (*Gets the canister of sugar and starts refilling the sugar bowl.*) I know he loved me.

MAMA. What if he did? It didn't change anything.

JESSIE. It didn't have to. I miss him.

MAMA. He never really went fishing, you know. Never once. His tackle box was full of chewing tobacco and all he ever did was drive out to the lake and sit in his car. Dawson told me. And Bennie at the bait shop, he told Dawson. They all laughed about it. And he'd come back from fishing and

33

all he'd have to show for it was . . . a whole pipe cleaner *family*—chickens, pigs, a dog with a bad leg—it was creepy strange. It made me sick to look at them, and I hid his pipe cleaners a couple of times but he always had more somewhere.

JESSIE. I thought it might be better for you after he died. You'd get interested in things. Breathe better. Change somehow.

MAMA. Into what? The Queen? A clerk in a shoestore? Why should I? Because he said to? Because you said to? (*Jessie shakes her head.*) Well, I wasn't here for his entertainment and I'm not here for yours either, Jessie. I don't know what I'm here for, but then I don't think about it. (*Realizing what all this means.*) But I bet you wouldn't be killing yourself if he were still alive. That's a fine thing to figure out, isn't it?

JESSIE. (*Filling the honey jar now.*) That's not true.

MAMA. Oh no? Then what were you asking about him for? Why did you want to know if I loved him?

JESSIE. I didn't think you did, that's all.

MAMA. Fine then. You were right. Do you feel better now?

JESSIE. (*Cleans the honey jar carefully.*) It feels good to be right about it.

MAMA. It didn't matter whether I loved him. It didn't matter to me and it didn't matter to him. And it didn't mean we didn't get along. It wasn't important. We didn't talk about it. (*Sweeping the pots off the cabinet.*) Take all these pots out to the porch!

JESSIE. What for?

MAMA. Just leave me this one pan. (*She jerks the silverware drawer open.*) Get me one knife, one fork, one big spoon and the can opener and put them out where I can get them. (*Starts throwing knives and forks in one of the pans.*)

JESSIE. Don't do that! I just straightened that drawer!

MAMA. (*Throws the pan in the sink.*) And throw out all the plates and cups. I'll use paper. Loretta can have what she

34

wants and Dawson can sell the rest.

JESSIE. (*Calmly.*) What are you doing?

MAMA. I'm not going to cook. I never liked it anyway. I like candy. Wrapped in plastic or coming in sacks. And tuna. I like tuna. I'll eat tuna, thank you.

JESSIE. (*Taking the pan out of the sink.*) What if you want to make apple butter? You can't make apple butter in that little pan. What if you leave carrots on cooking and burn up that pan?

MAMA. I don't like carrots.

JESSIE. What if the stawberries are good this year and you want to go picking with Agnes.

MAMA. I'll tell her to bring a pan. You said you would do whatever I wanted! I don't want a bunch of pans cluttering up my cabinets I can't get down to anyway. Throw them out. Every last one.

JESSIE. (*Gathering up the pots.*) I'm putting them all back in. I'm not taking them to the porch. If you want them, they'll be here. You'll bend down and get them, like you got the one for the cocoa. And if somebody else comes over here to cook they'll have something to cook in and that's the end of it!

MAMA. Who's going to come cook here?

JESSIE. Agnes.

MAMA. In my pots. Not on your life.

JESSIE. There's no reason why the two of you couldn't just live here together. Be cheaper for both of you and somebody to talk to. And if the birds bothered you, well, one day when Agnes is out getting her hair done, you could take them all for a walk!

MAMA. (*As Jessie straightens the silverware.*) So that's why you're pestering me about Agnes. You think you can rest easy if you get me a new babysitter. Well, I don't want to live with Agnes. I barely want to talk with Agnes. She's just around. We go back, that's all. I'm not letting Agnes near this place. You don't get off as easy as that, child.

JESSIE. O.K. then. It's just something to think about.

MAMA. I don't like things to think about. I like things to go on!

JESSIE. (*Closes the silverware drawer.*) I want to know what Daddy said to you the night he died. You came storming out of his room and said I could wait it out with him if I wanted to, but you were going to watch Gunsmoke. What did he say to you?

MAMA. He didn't have *anything* to say to me, Jessie. That's why I left. He didn't say a thing. It was his last chance not to talk to me and he took full advantage of it.

JESSIE. (*After a moment.*) I'm sorry you didn't love him. Sorry for you, I mean. He seemed like a nice man.

MAMA. (*As Jessie walks to the refrigerator.*) Ready for your apple now?

JESSIE. Soon as I'm through here, Mama.

MAMA. You won't like the apple either. It'll be just like the cocoa. You never liked eating at all, did you? Any of it! What have you been living on all these years, toothpaste?

JESSIE. (*As she starts to clean out the refrigerator.*) Now you know the milkman comes on Wednesdays and Saturdays and he leaves the order blank in an egg box and you give the bills to Dawson once a month.

MAMA. Do they still make that orangeade?

JESSIE. It's not orangeade, it's just orange.

MAMA. I'm going to get some. I thought they stopped making it. You just stopped ordering it.

JESSIE. You should drink milk.

MAMA. Not any more, I'm not. That hot chocolate was the last. Hooray.

JESSIE. (*Getting the garbage can from under the sink.*) I told them to keep delivering a quart a week no matter what you said. I told them you'd run out of cokes and you'd have to drink it. I told them I knew you wouldn't pour it on the ground . . .

MAMA. (*Finishing her sentence.*) And you told them you

36

weren't going to be ordering any more?

JESSIE. I told them I was taking a little holiday and to look after you.

MAMA. And they didn't think something was funny about that? You who doesn't go to the front steps? You, who only see the driveway looking down from a stretcher passed out cold?

JESSIE. (*Enjoying this, but not laughing.*) They said it was about time, but why didn't I take you with me. And I said I didn't think you'd want to go and they said, "Yeah, everybody's got their own idea of vacation."

MAMA. I guess you think that's funny.

JESSIE. (*Pulling jars out of the refrigerator.*) You know there never was any reason to call the ambulance for me. All they ever did for me in the emergency room was let me wake up. I could've done that here. Now, I'll just call them out and you say yes or no. I know you like pickles. Ketchup?

MAMA. Keep it.

JESSIE. We've had this since last Fourth of July.

MAMA. Keep the ketchup. Keep it all.

JESSIE. Are you going to drink ketchup from the bottle or what? How can you want your food and not want your pots to cook it in? This stuff will all spoil in here, Mother.

MAMA. Nothing I ever did was good enough for you and I want to know why.

JESSIE. That's not true.

MAMA. And I want to know why you've lived here this long feeling the way you do.

JESSIE. You have no earthly idea how I feel.

MAMA. Well how could I? You're real far back there, Jessie.

JESSIE. Back where?

MAMA. What's it like over there, where you are? Do people always say the right thing or get whatever they want or what?

JESSIE. What are you talking about?

MAMA. Why do you read the newspaper? Why don't you wear that sweater I made for you? Do you remember how I used to look or am I just any old woman now? When you have a fit do you see stars or what? How did you fall off the horse, really? Why did Cecil leave you? Where did you put my old glasses?

JESSIE. (*Stunned by Mama's intensity.*) They're in the bottom drawer of your dresser in an old Milk of Magnesia box. Cecil left me because he made me choose between him and smoking.

MAMA. Jessie, I know he wasn't that dumb.

JESSIE. I never understood why he hated it so much when it's so good. Smoking is the only thing I know that's always just what you think it's going to be. Just like it was the last time and right there when you want it and real quiet.

MAMA. Your fits made him sick and you know it.

JESSIE. Say seizures, not fits. Seizures.

MAMA. It's the same thing. A seizure in the hospital is a fit at home.

JESSIE. They didn't bother him at all. Except he did feel responsible for it. It *was* his idea to go horseback riding that day. It was his idea I could do *anything* if I just made up my mind to. I fell off the horse because I didn't know how to hold on. Cecil left for pretty much the same reason.

MAMA. He had a girl, Jessie. I walked right in on them in the tool shed.

JESSIE. (*After a moment.*) O.K. That's fair. (*Lights another cigarette.*) Was she very pretty?

MAMA. She was Agnes' girl, Carlene. Judge for yourself.

JESSIE. (*As she walks to the living room.*) I guess you and Agnes had a good talk about that, huh?

MAMA. I never thought he was good enough for you. They moved here from Tennessee, you know.

JESSIE. What are you talking about? You liked him better than I did. You flirted him out here to build your porch or I'd never even met him at all. You thought maybe he'd help you out around the place, come in and get some coffee and

38

talk to you. God knows what you thought. All that curly hair.

MAMA. He's the best carpenter I ever saw. That little house of yours will still be standing at the end of the world, Jessie.

JESSIE. You didn't need a porch, Mama.

MAMA. All right! I wanted you to have a husband.

JESSIE. And I couldn't get one on my own, of course.

MAMA. How were you going to get a husband never opening your mouth to a living soul?

JESSIE. So I was quiet about it, so what?

MAMA. So I should have let you just sit here? Sit like your Daddy? Sit here?

JESSIE. Maybe.

MAMA. Well I didn't think so.

JESSIE. Well what did you know?

MAMA. I never said I knew much. How was I supposed to learn anything living out here? I didn't know enough to do half the things I did in my life. Things happen. You do what you can about them and you see what happens next. I married you off to the wrong man, I admit that. So I took you in when he left. I'm sorry.

JESSIE. He wasn't the wrong man.

MAMA. He didn't love you, Jessie, or he wouldn't have left.

JESSIE. He wasn't the wrong man, Mama. I loved Cecil so much. And I tried to get more exercise and I tried to stay awake. I tried to learn to ride a horse. And I tried to stay outside with him, and but he always knew I was trying so it didn't work.

MAMA. He was a selfish man. He told me once he hated to see people move into his houses after he built them. He knew they'd mess them up.

JESSIE. I loved that bridge he built over the creek in back of the house. It didn't have to be anything special, a couple of boards would have been just fine, but he used that yellow pine and rubbed it so smooth . . .

MAMA. He had responsibilities here. He had a wife and son here and he failed you.

JESSIE. Or that baby bed he built for Ricky. I told him he didn't have to spend so much time on it, but he said it had to last and the thing ended up weighing 200 pounds and I couldn't move it. I said, "How long did a baby bed have to last anyway?" But maybe he thought if it was strong enough, it might keep Ricky a baby.

MAMA. Ricky is too much like Cecil.

JESSIE. He is not. Ricky is as much like me as it's possible for any human to be. We even wear the same size pants. These are his, I think.

MAMA. That's just the same size. That's not you're the same person.

JESSIE. I see it on his face. I hear it when he talks. We look out at the world and we see the same thing. Not Fair. And the only difference between us is Ricky's out there trying to get even. And he knows not to trust anybody and he got it straight from me. And he knows not to try to get work and guess where he got that. And he walks around like there's loose boards in the floor and you know who laid that floor, I did.

MAMA. Ricky isn't through yet. You don't know how he'll turn out!

JESSIE. (*Going back to the kitchen.*) Yes I do and so did Cecil. Ricky is the two of us together for all time in too small a space. And we're tearing each other apart, like always, inside that boy and if you don't see it, then you're just blind.

MAMA. Give him time, Jess.

JESSIE. Oh, he'll have plenty of that. 5 years for forgery, 10 years for armed assault . . .

MAMA. (*Furious.*) Stop that! (*Then pleading.*) Jessie, Cecil might be ready to try it again, honey, that happens sometimes. Go downtown. Find him. Talk to him. He didn't know what he had in you. Maybe he sees things different

40

now, but you're not going to know that til you go see him. Or call him up! Right now! He might be home.

JESSIE. And say what? Nothing's changed, Cecil, I'd just like to look at you, if you don't mind? No. He loved me, Mama. He just didn't know how things fall down around me like they do. I think he did the right thing. He gave himself another chance, that's all. But I did beg him to take me with him. I did tell him I would leave Ricky and you and everything I loved out here if only he would take me with him, but he couldn't and I understand that. (*A pause.*) I wrote that note I showed you. I wrote it. Not Cecil. I said "I'm sorry, Jessie, I can't fix it all for you." I said I'd always love me, not Cecil. But that's how he felt.

MAMA. Then he should've taken you with him!

JESSIE. (*Picking up the garbage bag she has filled.*) Mama, you don't pack your garbage when you move.

MAMA. You will not call yourself garbage, Jessie.

JESSIE. (*Taking the bag to the big garbage can.*) Just a way of saying it, Mama. Thinking about my list, that's all. (*Opening the can, putting the garbage in, then securing the lid.*) Well, a little more than that. I was trying to say it's all right that Cecil left. It was . . . a relief in a way. I never was what he wanted to see, so it was better when he wasn't looking at me all the time.

MAMA. I'll make your apple now.

JESSIE. No thanks. You get the manicure stuff and I'll be right there. (*Jessie ties up the big garbage bag in the can and replaces the small garbage bag under the sink, all the time trying desperately to regain her calm. Mama watches, from a distance, her hand reaching unconsciously for the phone. Then she has a better idea. Or rather she thinks of the only other thing left and is willing to try it. Maybe she is even convinced it will work.*)

MAMA. Jessie, I think your Daddy had little . . .

JESSIE. (*Interrupting her.*) Garbage night is Tuesday. Put it out as late as you can. The Davis's dogs get in it if you don't.

41

(*Now replacing the garbage sack in the can under the sink.*)
And keep ordering the heavy black bags. It doesn't pay to
buy the cheap ones. And I've got all the ties here with the
hammers and all. Take them out of the box as soon as you
open a new one and put them in this drawer. They'll get lost
if you don't and rubber bands or something else won't work.
MAMA. I think your Daddy had fits too. I think he sat in
his chair and had little fits. I read this a long time ago in a
magazine, how little fits go, just little blackouts where maybe
their eyes don't even close and people just call them "thinking spells."
JESSIE. (*Getting the slipcover out the laundry basket.*) I
don't think you want this manicure we've been looking for-
ward to. I washed this cover for the sofa, but it'll take both
of us to get it back on.
MAMA. I watched his eyes. I know that's what it was. The
magazine said some people don't even know they've had one.
JESSIE. Daddy would've known if he'd had fits, Mama.
MAMA. The lady in this story kept track of her fits and she'd
had 80,000 of them in the last eleven years.
JESSIE. Next time you wash this cover, it'll dry better if you
put it on wet.
MAMA. Jessie, listen to what I'm telling you. This lady had
anywhere between five and five hundred fits a day and they
lasted maybe 15 seconds apiece, so that out of her life, she'd
only lost about two weeks altogether and she had a full-time
secretary job and an I.Q. of 120.
JESSIE. (*Has to be amused by Mama's approach.*) You want
to talk about fits, is that it?
MAMA. Yes. I do. I want to say . . .
JESSIE. (*Interrupting.*) Most of the time I wouldn't even
know I'd had one, except I wake up with different clothes on
feeling like I've been run over. Sometimes I feel my head
start to turn around or hear myself scream. And sometimes,
there *is* this dizzy stupid feeling a little before it, but if the
TV's on, well, it's easy to miss. (*As Jessie and Mama replace*

42

the slip cover on the sofa and the afghan on the chair, the physical struggle somehow mirrors the emotional one in the conversation.)

MAMA. I can tell when you're about to have one. Your eyes get this big! But Jessie, you haven't . . .

JESSIE. (*Taking charge of this.*) What do they look like? The seizures.

MAMA. (*Reluctant.*) Different each time, Jess.

JESSIE. O.K. Pick one, then. A good one. I think I want to know now.

MAMA. There's not much to tell. You just . . . crumple, in a heap, like a puppet and somebody cut the strings all at once, or like the firing squad in some Mexican movie, you just slide down the wall, you know. You don't know what happens? How can you not know what happens?

JESSIE. I'm busy.

MAMA. That's not funny.

JESSIE. I'm not laughing. My head turns around and I fall down and then what?

MAMA. Well, your chest squeezes in and out and you sound like you're gagging, sucking air in and out like you can't breathe.

JESSIE. Do it for me. Make the sound for me.

MAMA. I will not. It's awful sounding.

JESSIE. Yeah. It felt like it might be. What's next.

MAMA. Your mouth bites down and I have to get your tongue out of the way fast so you don't bite yourself.

JESSIE. Or you. I bite you too, don't I?

MAMA. You got me once real good. I had to get a tetanus! But I know what to watch for now. Then you turn blue and the jerks start up. Like I'm standing there poking you with a cattle prod or you're sticking your finger in a light socket as fast as you can.

JESSIE. Foaming like a mad dog the whole time.

MAMA. It's bubbling, Jess, not foam like the washer overflowed, for God's sake, it's bubbling like a baby spitting

43

up. I go get a wet washcloth, that's all. And then the jerks slow down and you wet yourself and it's over. Two minutes tops.

JESSIE. How do I get to the bed?

MAMA. How do you think?

JESSIE. I'm too heavy for you now. How do you do it?

MAMA. I call Dawson. But I get you cleaned up before he gets here and I make him leave before you wake up.

JESSIE. You could just leave me on the floor.

MAMA. I want you to wake up someplace nice, O.K.? (*Then making a real effort.*) But Jessie, and this is the reason I even brought this up! You haven't had a seizure for a solid year. A whole year, do you realize that?

JESSIE. Yeah, the phenobarb's about right now, I guess.

MAMA. You bet it is. You might never have another one, ever! You might be through with it for all time!

JESSIE. Could be.

MAMA. You are. I know you are!

JESSIE. I sure am feeling good. I really am. The double vision's gone and my gums aren't swelling. No rashes or anything. I'm feeling as good as I ever felt in my life. I'm even feeling like worrying or getting mad and I'm not afraid it will start a fit if I do. I just go ahead.

MAMA. Of course you do! You can even scream at me, if you want to. I can take it. You don't have to act like you're just visiting here, Jessie. This is your house too.

JESSIE. The best part is my memory's back.

MAMA. Your memory's always been good. When couldn't you remember things? You're always reminding me what . . .

JESSIE. Because I've made lists for everything. But now, I remember what things mean on my lists. I see dishtowels and I used to wonder whether I was supposed to wash them, buy them or look for them because I wouldn't remember where I put them after I washed them, but now I know it means wrap them up, they're a present for Loretta's birthday.

44

MAMA. (*Finished with the sofa now.*) You used to go looking for your lists, too, I've noticed that. You always know where they are now! (*Then suddenly worried.*) Loretta's birthday isn't coming up, is it?

JESSIE. I made a list of all the birthdays for you. I even put yours on it. (*A small smile.*) So you can call Loretta and remind her.

MAMA. Let's take Loretta to Howard Johnson's and have those fried clams. I *know* you love that clam roll.

JESSIE. (*A slight pause.*) I won't be here, Mama.

MAMA. What have we just been talking about? You'll be here. You're well, Jessie. You're starting all over. You said it yourself. You're remembering things and . . .

JESSIE. I won't be here. If I'd ever had a year like this, to think straight and all, before now, I'd be gone already.

MAMA. (*Not pleading, commanding.*) No, Jessie.

JESSIE. (*Folding the rest of the laundry.*) Yes, Mama. Once I started remembering, I could see what it all added up to.

MAMA. The fits are over!

JESSIE. It's not the fits, Mama.

MAMA. Then it's me for giving them to you, but I didn't do it!

JESSIE. It's not the fits! You said it yourself, the medicine takes care of the fits.

MAMA. (*Interrupting.*) Your Daddy gave you those fits, Jessie. He passed it down to you like your green eyes and your straight hair. It's not my fault!

JESSIE. So what if he had little fits? It's not inherited. I fell off the horse. It was an accident.

MAMA. The horse wasn't the first time, Jessie. You had a fit when you were five years old.

JESSIE. I did not.

MAMA. You did! You were eating a popsicle and down you went. He gave it to you. It's *his* fault, not mine.

JESSIE. Well, you took your time telling me.

MAMA. How do you tell that to a five year old?

45

JESSIE. What did the doctor say?

MAMA. He said kids have them all the time. He said there wasn't anything to do but wait for another one.

JESSIE. But I didn't have another one. (*Now there is a real silence.*) You mean to tell me I had fits all the time as a kid and you just told me I fell down or something and it wasn't til I had the fit when Cecil was looking that anybody bothered to find out what was the matter with me?

MAMA. It wasn't *all the time*, Jessie, and they changed when you started to school, more like your Daddy's. Oh, that was some swell time, sitting here with the two of you turning on and off like lightbulbs some nights.

JESSIE. How many fits did I have?

MAMA. You never hurt yourself. I never let you out of my sight. I caught you every time.

JESSIE. But you didn't tell anybody.

MAMA. It was none of their business.

JESSIE. You were ashamed.

MAMA. I didn't want anybody to know. Least of all you.

JESSIE. Least of all, me. Oh right. That was mine to know, Mama, not yours. Did Daddy know?

MAMA. He thought you were . . . you fell down a lot. That's what he thought. You were careless. Or maybe he thought I beat you. I don't know what he thought. He didn't think about it.

JESSIE. Because you didn't tell him!

MAMA. If I told him about you, I'd have to tell him about him!

JESSIE. I don't like this. I don't like this one bit.

MAMA. I didn't think you'd like it. That's why I didn't tell you.

JESSIE. If I'd known I was an epileptic, Mama, I wouldn't have ridden any horses.

MAMA. Make you feel like a freak, is that what I should have done?

JESSIE. Just get the manicure tray and sit down!

46

MAMA. (*Throwing it to the floor.*) I don't want a manicure!

JESSIE. Doesn't look like you do, no.

MAMA. Maybe I did drop you, you don't know.

JESSIE. If you say you didn't, you didn't.

MAMA. (*Beginning to break down.*) Maybe I fed you the wrong thing. Maybe you had a fever some time and I didn't know it soon enough. Maybe it's a punishment.

JESSIE. For what?

MAMA. I don't know. Because of how I felt about your father. Because I didn't want any more children. Because I smoked too much or didn't eat right when I was carrying you. It has to be something I did.

JESSIE. It does not. It's just a sickness, not a curse. Epilepsy doesn't mean anything. It just is.

MAMA. I'm not talking about the fits here, Jessie! I'm talking about this killing yourself. It has to be me that's the matter here. You wouldn't be doing this if it wasn't. I didn't tell you things or I married you off to the wrong man or I took you in and let your life get away from you or all of it put together. I don't know what I did, but I did it, I know. This is all my fault, Jessie, but I don't know what to do about it, now!

JESSIE. (*Exasperated at having to say this again.*) It doesn't have anything to do with you!

MAMA. Everything you do has to do with me, Jessie. You can't do *anything*, wash your face or cut your finger, without doing it to me. That's right! You might as well kill me as you, Jessie, it's the same thing. This has to do with me, Jessie.

JESSIE. Then what if it does! What if it has everything to do with you! What if you are all I have and you're not enough? What if I could take all the rest of it if only I didn't have you here? What if the only way I can get away from you for good is to kill myself? What if it is? I can *still* do it!

MAMA. (*In desperate tears.*) Don't leave me, Jessie! (*Jessie stands for a moment, then turns for the bedroom.*) No! (*Mama grabs her arm.*)

47

JESSIE. (*Carefully takes her arm away.*) I have a box of things I want people to have. I'm just going to go get it for you. You . . . just rest a minute. (*And Jessie is gone and Mama heads for the telephone, but she can't even pick up the receiver this time, and instead, stoops to clean up the bottles that have spilled out of the tray. Jessie returns carrying a box that groceries were delivered in. It probably says Hershey Kisses or Starkist Tuna. Mama is still down on the floor cleaning up, hoping that maybe if she just makes it look nice enough, Jessie will stay.*)

MAMA. Jessie, how can I live here without you? I need you! You're supposed to tell me to stand up straight and say how nice I look in my pink dress and drink my milk. You're supposed to go around and lock up so I know we're safe for the night, and when I wake up, you're supposed to be out there making the coffee and watching me get older every day and you're supposed to help me die when the time comes. I can't do that by myself, Jessie. I'm not like you, Jessie. I hate the quiet and I don't want to die and I don't want you to go, Jessie. How can I . . . (*Has to stop a moment.*) How can I get up every day knowing you had to kill yourself to make it stop hurting and I was here all the time and I never even saw it. And then you gave me this chance to make it better, convince you to stay alive and I couldn't do it. How can I live with myself after this, Jessie?

JESSIE. I only told you so I could explain it, so you wouldn't blame yourself, so you wouldn't feel bad. There wasn't anything you could say to change my mind. I didn't want you to save me. I just wanted you to know.

MAMA. Stay with me just a little longer. Just a few more years. I don't have that many more to go, Jessie. And as soon as I'm dead, you can do whatever you want. Maybe with me gone, you'll have all the quiet you want, right here in the house. And maybe one day you'll put in some begonias up the walk and get just the right rain for them all summer. And Ricky will be married by then and he'll bring your grandbabies over and you can sneak them a piece of candy when their Daddy's not looking and then be real glad when they've gone home and left you to your quiet again.

JESSIE. Don't you see, Mama, everything I do winds up like this. How could I think you would understand? How could I think you would want a manicure? We could hold hands for an hour and then I could go shoot myself? I'm sorry about tonight, Mama, but it's exactly why I'm doing it.

MAMA. If you've got the guts to kill yourself, Jessie, you've got the guts to stay alive.

JESSIE. I know that. So it's really just a matter of where I'd rather be.

MAMA. Look, maybe I can't think of what you should do, but that doesn't mean there isn't something that would help. *You* find it. *You* think of it. You can keep trying. You can get brave and try some more. You don't have to give up!

JESSIE. I'm *not* giving up! This *is* the other thing I'm trying. And I'm sure there are some other things that might work, but *might* work isn't good enough any more. I need something that *will* work. *This* will work. That's why I picked it.

MAMA. But something might happen. Something that could change everything. Who knows what it might be, but it might be worth waiting for! (*Jessie doesn't respond.*) Try it for two more weeks. We could have more talks like tonight.

JESSIE. No, Mama.

MAMA. I'll pay more attention to you. Tell the truth when you ask me. Let you have your say.

JESSIE. No, Mama! We wouldn't have more talks like tonight, because it's this next part that's made this last part so good, Mama. No, Mama. *This* is how I have my say. This is how I say what I thought about it *all* and I say No. To Dawson and Loretta and the Red Chinese and epilepsy and Ricky and Cecil and you. And me. And hope. I say No! (*Then going to Mama on the sofa.*) Just let me go easy, Mama.

49

MAMA. How can I let you go?

JESSIE. You can because you have to. It's what you've always done.

MAMA. You are my child!

JESSIE. I am what became of your child. (*Mama cannot answer.*) I found an old baby picture of me. And it was somebody else, not me. It was somebody pink and fat who never heard of sick or lonely, somebody who cried and got fed, and reached up and got held and kicked but didn't hurt anybody, and slept whenever she wanted to, just by closing her eyes. Somebody who mainly just laid there and laughed at the colors waving around over her head and chewed on a polka-dot whale and woke up knowing some new trick nearly every day and rolled over and drooled on the sheet and felt your hand pulling my quilt back up over me. That's who I started out and this is who is left. (*There is no self-pity here.*) That's what this is about. It's somebody I lost, all right, it's my own self. Who I never was. Or who I tried to be and never got there. Somebody I waited for who never came. And never will. So, see, it doesn't much matter what else happens in the world or in this house, even. I'm what was worth waiting for and I didn't make it. Me . . . who might have made a difference to me . . . I'm not going to show up, so there's no reason to stay, except to keep you company, and that's . . . not reason enough because I'm not . . . very good company. (*A pause.*) Am I.

MAMA. (*Knowing she must tell the truth.*) No. And neither am I.

JESSIE. I had this strange little thought, well, maybe it's not so strange. Anyway, after Christmas, after I decided to do this, I would wonder, sometimes, what might keep me here, what might be worth staying for, and you know what it was? It was maybe if there was something I really liked, like maybe if I really liked rice pudding or cornflakes for breakfast or something, that might be enough.

MAMA. Rice pudding is good.

JESSIE. Not to me.

MAMA. And you're not afraid?

JESSIE. Afraid of what?

MAMA. I'm afraid of it, for me, I mean. When my time comes. I know it's coming, but . . .

JESSIE. You don't know when. Like in a scary movie.

MAMA. Yeah, sneaking up on me like some killer on the loose, hiding out in the back yard just waiting for me to have my hands full some day and how am I supposed to protect myself anyhow when I don't know what he looks like and I don't know how he sounds coming up behind me like that or if it will hurt or take very long or what I don't get done before it happens.

JESSIE. You've got plenty of time left.

MAMA. I forget what for, right now.

JESSIE. For whatever happens, I don't know. For the rest of your life. For Agnes burning down one more house or Dawson losing his hair or . . .

MAMA. (*Quickly.*) Jessie. I can't just sit here and say O.K., kill yourself if you want to.

JESSIE. Sure you can. You just did. Say it again.

MAMA. (*Really startled.*) Jessie! (*Quiet horror.*) How dare you! (*Furious.*) How dare you! You think you can just leave whenever you want like you're watching television here? No, you can't, Jessie. You make me feel like a fool for being alive, child and you are so wrong! I like it here, and I will stay here until they make me go, until they drag me screaming and I mean screeching into my grave and you're real smart to get away before then because, I mean, honey, you've never heard noise like that in your life. (*Jessie turns away.*) Who am I talking to? You're gone already, aren't you? I'm looking right through you! I can't stop you because you're already gone! I guess you think they'll all have to talk about you now! I guess you think this will really confuse them. Oh yes, ever since Christmas, you've been laughing to yourself and thinking, "Boy are they all in for a surprise." Well, nobody's going to

51

be a bit surprised, sweetheart. This is just like you. Do it the hard way, that's my girl all right. (*Jessie gets up and goes into the kitchen, but Mama follows her.*) You know who they're going to feel sorry for? Me! How about that! Not you, me! They're going to be *ashamed* of you. Yes. *Ashamed!* If somebody asks Dawson about it, he'll change the subject as fast as he can. He'll talk about how much he has to pay to park his car these days.

JESSIE. Leave me alone.

MAMA. It's the truth!

JESSIE. I should've just left you a note!

MAMA. (*Screaming.*) Yes! (*Then suddenly understanding what she has said, nearly paralyzed by the thought of it, she turns slowly to face Jessie, nearly whispering.*) No. No. I . . . might not have thought of all the things you've said.

JESSIE. It's O.K., Mama. (*And Mama is nearly unconscious from the emotional devastation of these last few moments. She sits down at the kitchen table, hurt and angry and so desperately afraid. But she looks almost numb. She is so far beyond what is known as pain that she is virtually unreachable and Jessie knows this, and talks quietly, watching for signs of recovery. She washes her hands in the sink.*) I remember you liked that preacher who did Daddy's, so if you want to ask him to do the service, that's O.K. with me.

MAMA. (*Not an answer, just a word.*) What.

JESSIE. (*Putting on hand lotion as she talks.*) And pick some songs you like or let Agnes pick, she'll know exactly which ones. Oh and I had your dress cleaned that you wore to Daddy's. You looked real good in that.

MAMA. I don't remember, hon.

JESSIE. And it won't be so bad once your friends start coming to the funeral home. You'll probably see people you haven't seen for years, but I thought about what you should say to get you over that nervous part when they first come in.

MAMA. (*Simply repeating.*) Come in.

JESSIE. Take them up to see their flowers, they'd like that.

And when they say, "I'm so sorry, Thelma," you just say, "I appreciate your coming, Connie." And then ask how their garden was this summer or what they're doing for Thanksgiving or how their children . . .

MAMA. I don't think I should ask about their children. I'll talk about what they have on, that's always good. And I'll have some crochet work with me.

JESSIE. And Agnes will be there, so you might not have to talk at all.

MAMA. Maybe if Connie Richards does come, I can get her to tell me where she gets that Irish yarn, she calls it. I know it doesn't come from Ireland. I think it just comes with a green wrapper.

JESSIE. And be sure to invite enough people home afterward so you get enough food to feed them all and have some left for you. But don't let anybody take anything home, especially Loretta.

MAMA. Loretta will get all the food set up, honey. It's only fair to let her have some macaroni or something.

JESSIE. No, Mama. You have to be more selfish from now on. (*Sitting down now with Mama.*) Now, somebody's bound to ask you why I did it and you just say you don't know. That you loved me and you know I loved you and we just sat around tonight like every other night of our lives and then I came over and kissed you and said, " 'Night, Mother," and you heard me close my bedroom door and the next thing you heard was the shot. And whatever reasons I had, well, you guess I just took them with me.

MAMA. (*Quietly.*) It was something personal.

JESSIE. Good. That's good, Mama.

MAMA. That's what I'll say, then.

JESSIE. Personal. Yeah.

MAMA. Is that what I tell Dawson and Loretta too? We sat around, you kissed me, " 'Night, Mother?" They'll want to know more, Jessie. They won't believe it.

JESSIE. Well, then, tell them what we did. I filled up the

53

candy jars. I cleaned out the refrigerator. We made some hot chocolate and put the cover back on the sofa. You had no idea. All right? I really think it's better that way. If they know we talked about it, they really won't understand how you let me go. (*Mama does not answer.*) It's private. Tonight is private, yours and mine, and I don't want anybody else to have any of it.

MAMA. O.K. then.

JESSIE. (*Standing behind Mama now, holding her shoulders.*) Now, when you hear the shot, I don't want you to come in. First of all, you won't be able to get in by yourself, but I don't want you trying. Call Dawson, then call the police and then call Agnes. And then you'll need something to do til somebody gets here, so wash the hot chocolate pan. You wash that pan til you hear the doorbell ring and I don't care if it's an hour, you keep washing that pan.

MAMA. I'll make my calls and then I'll just sit. I won't need something to do. What will the police say?

JESSIE. They'll do that gunpowder test, and ask you what happened and by that time, the ambulance will be here and they'll come in and get me and you know how that goes. You stay out here with Dawson and Loretta. You keep Dawson out here. I want the police in the room first, not Dawson, O.K.?

MAMA. What if Dawson and Loretta want me to go home with them?

JESSIE. (*Returning to the living room.*) That's up to you.

MAMA. I think I'll stay here. All they've got is Sanka.

JESSIE. Maybe Agnes could come stay with you for a few days.

MAMA. (*Standing up now, looking into the living room.*) I'd rather be by myself, I think. (*Walking toward the box Jessie brought in earlier.*) You want me to give people those things?

JESSIE. (*They sit down on the sofa, Jessie holding the box on her lap.*) I want Loretta to have my little calculator. Dawson bought it for himself, you know, but then he saw one he liked better and he couldn't bring both of them home with Loretta counting every penny the way she does, so he gave the first one to me. Be funny for her to have it now, don't you think? And all my house slippers are in a sack for her in my closet. Tell her I know they'll fit and I've never worn any of them and make sure Dawson hears you tell her that. I'm glad he loves Loretta so much, but I wish he knew not everybody has her size feet.

MAMA. (*Taking the calculator.*) O.K.

JESSIE. (*Reaching into the box again.*) This letter is for Dawson, but it's mostly about you, so read it if you want. There's a list of presents for you for at least twenty more Christmases and birthdays, so if you want anything special you better add it to this list before you give it to him. Or if you want to be surprised, just don't read that page. This Christmas, you're getting mostly stuff for the house like a new rug in your bathroom and needlework, but next Christmas, you're really going to cost him next Christmas. I think you'll like it a lot and you'd never think of it.

MAMA. And you think he'll go for it?

JESSIE. I think he'll feel like a real jerk if he doesn't. Me telling him to like this and all. Now, this number's where you call Cecil. I called it last week and he answered so I know he still lives there.

MAMA. What do you want me to tell him?

JESSIE. Tell him we talked about him and I only had good things to say about him, but mainly tell him to find Ricky and tell him what I did and tell Ricky you have something for him, out here, from me, and to come get it. (*Pulls a sack out of the box.*)

MAMA. (*The sack feels empty.*) What is it?

JESSIE. (*Taking it off.*) My watch. (*Putting it in the sack and taking a ribbon out of the sack to tie around the top of it.*)

MAMA. He'll sell it!

JESSIE. That's the idea. I appreciate him not stealing it already. I'd like to buy him a good meal.

MAMA. He'll buy dope with it!

JESSIE. Well, then, I hope he gets some good dope with it, Mama. And the rest of this is for you. (*Handing Mama the box now. Mama picks up the things and looks at them.*)

MAMA. (*Surprised and pleased.*) When did you do all this? During my naps, I guess.

JESSIE. I guess. I tried to be quiet about it. (*As Mama is puzzled by the presents.*) Those are just little presents. For whenever you need one. They're not bought presents, just things I thought you might like to look at, pictures, or things you think you've lost. Things you didn't know you had, even. You'll see.

MAMA. I'm not sure I want them. They'll make me think of you.

JESSIE. No they won't. They're just things, like a free tube of toothpaste I found hanging on the door one day.

MAMA. Oh. All right then.

JESSIE. Well, maybe there's one nice present in there somewhere. It's Granny's ring she gave me and I thought you might like to have it, but I didn't think you'd wear it if I gave it to you right now.

MAMA. (*Taking the box to a table nearby.*) No. Probably not. (*Turning back to face her.*) I'm ready for my manicure, I guess. Want me to wash my hands again?

JESSIE. (*Standing up.*) It's time for me to go, Mama.

MAMA. (*Starting to her.*) No, Jessie, you've got all night!

JESSIE. (*As Mama grabs her.*) No, Mama.

MAMA. It's not even ten o'clock.

JESSIE. (*Very calm.*) Let me go, Mama.

MAMA. I can't. You can't go. You can't do this. You didn't say it would be so soon, Jessie. I'm scared. I love you.

JESSIE. (*Takes her hands away.*) Let go of me, Mama. I've said everything I had to say.

MAMA. (*Standing still a minute.*) You said you wanted to do my nails.

JESSIE. (*Taking a small step backward.*) I can't. It's too late.

MAMA. It's not too late!

JESSIE. I don't want you to wake Dawson and Loretta when you call. I want them to still be up and dressed so they can get right over.

MAMA. (*As Jessie backs up, Mama moves in on her, but carefully.*) They wake up fast, Jessie, if they have to. They don't matter here, Jessie. You do. I do. We're not through yet. We've got a lot of things to take care of here. I don't know where my prescriptions are and you didn't tell me what to tell Doctor Davis when he calls or how much you want me to tell Ricky or who I call to rake the leaves or . . .

JESSIE. Don't try and stop me, Mama, you can't do it.

MAMA. (*Grabs her again, this time hard.*) I can too! I'll stand in front of this hall and you can't get past me. (*They struggle.*) You'll have to knock me down to get away from me, Jessie. I'm not about to let you . . . (*Mama struggles with Jessie at the door an in the struggle, Jessie gets away from her and:*)

JESSIE. (*Almost a whisper.*) 'Night, Mother. (*Jessie vanishes into her bedroom and we hear the door lock just as Mama gets to it.*)

MAMA. (*Screams.*) Jessie! (*And pounds on the door.*) Jessie, you let me in there. Don't you do this, Jessie. I'm not going to stop screaming until you open this door, Jessie. Jessie! Jessie! What if I don't do any of the things you told me to do! I'll tell Cecil what a miserable man he was to make you feel the way he did and I'll give Ricky's watch to Dawson if I feel like it and the only way you can make sure I do what you want is you come out here and make me, Jessie! (*Pounding again.*) Jessie! Stop this! I didn't know! I was here with you all the time. How could I know you were so alone? (*And Mama stops for a moment, breathless and frantic, putting her ear to the door and when she doesn't hear anything, she*) *stands back up straight again and screams once more.*) Jessie! Please! (*And we hear the shot, and it sounds like an answer, it sounds like No. And Mama collapses against the door, tears streaming down her face, but not screaming any more. In shock now.*) Jessie, Jessie, child . . . Forgive me. (*A pause.*) I thought you were mine. (*And she leaves the door and makes her way through the living room, around the furniture, as though she didn't know where it was, not knowing what to do. Finally, she goes to the stove in the kitchen and picks up the hot chocolate pan and carries it with her to the telephone and holds onto it while she dials the number. She looks down at the pan, holding it tight like her life depended on it. She hears Loretta answer.*) Loretta, let me talk to Dawson, honey.

THE END

PROPERTY PLOT

KITCHEN

Percolator
Spices & spice rack
Hand lotion
Dish soap
Paper towels & rack
Dish drainer
Potholders & mitts
Soap dish
Dish rag & rack
Sponge
Metal garbage can w/pedal
Salt & pepper shaker
Stove
Double sink
Refrigerator
Stove hood exhaust
2 candy dishes (in drainer)
Toaster & cover
Mixmaster
Radio
Mug of pencils & pens
Cook books

Dial telephone
Memoboard
Phone book (thin)
Assorted terra cotta bowls
Assorted wicker baskets
Assorted small appliances
Soda syphon
Honey bear
Assorted plastic bowls
Wooden tray
Knife rack
Napkin holder (w/folded napkins)
Pitcher & bowl
Assorted dish towels
Sugar bowl w/spoon
Cannister set
Cookie jar
Kitchen table w/2 chairs
Loud wind up clock
Hanging lamp over kitchen table
Rubbermaid sink stop
Magic marker
Address book
Wicker basket w/6"knitting and pre-measured 6" cloth tape
and knitting equipment
Ashtray

Refrigerator: (main compartment)
    Assorted jars, cans, cartons & Tupperware
    Milk
    Catsup
    Pickles
    Cream cheese (used & spoiled)
    Sour cream (used & spoiled)
    Cottage cheese (used & spoiled)

Cheese whiz (used & spoiled)
Chocolate syrup (used & spoiled)

Refrigerator: (crisper)
  Celery stalks—wilted
  Cucumber (½ in baggie)
  Lettuce leaves—wilted

Cabinets:
  Assorted plates, cups & saucers, bowls, glassware
  Canned goods, boxes
  Can of cocoa
  Bag of marshmallows
  Bag of caramels
  Clear plastic sacks of wrapped candy
  Can of tuna
  Snowballs (½ empty)
  1 mixing cup (for cocoa)
  2 cups & saucers (for cocoa)
  6 coffee bag sacks:
      1 chocolate kisses
      1 hard candy
      1 chewy mint
      1 chocolate covered cherries
      1 red hots
      1 caramels
  4 large pill jars (w/prescription labels for Thelma Cates) ⅔
filled with pills
  4 small prescription bottles w/Thelma Cates labels-empty
  1 small prescription bottle w/Jessie Cates label- ⅔ full
  1 hand towel to catch spilled pills

Cupboards:
  6 assorted sauce pans

Stewpot w/cover
Plastic trash container (under sink)
Box of small white plastic garbage bags (sink can)
Box of large black plastic garbage bags (pedal can)
Cleaning supplies

Drawers:
Assorted silverware in rubbermaid tray
4 placemats
1 large spoon (wooden)
1 large can opener (plastic handles)
1 measuring spoon
Hammer & lock ties (black garbage bags)
Peel off wire ties (white garbage bags)
Extention cord
Bic lighter
Sand paper
Masking tape
Elmer's glue
Thumbtacks
Batteries

NOTE: all food, cleaning supply, refrigerator and candy props should be national brands which do not indicate any specific area in the country.

PROPERTY LIST

LIVING ROOM

2 cushion sofa w/Afghan over back
Oblong drop leaf table behind sofa
Buffet table—candy bowl w/8 caramel wrappers & 1 caramel
2 tall bar stools
1 chair (matching to kitchen chairs)
TV on rolling stand
Corner hutch
Sewing table—empty chewy mint bowl
Upholstered arm chair—crochet & needle on seat
Arm chair side table
Sofa side table

Arm chair side table: on top—
  Wind up clock
  Embroidery
  Mama's glasses (½ moon)
  Small table lamp
Arm chair side table: in open shelf—
  Magazines
  Newspapers opened to crossword puzzles

Sofa side table:
  Manicure tray w/4 bottles of polish, plastic bottle

Nail polish remover, 2 folded Kleenex, nail files,
Cuticle sticks, metal finger bowl
Eyeglass cleaning spray
TV Guide (opened to Saturday evening)
Magnifying glass
Candy bowl w/4 chocolate kiss wrappers

Oblong drop leaf table:
Embroidered sewing basket w/towel inside
Whitman Sampler candy box w/chocolates & 4 empty
wrappers

Laundry basket: (filled in layers from bottom to top)
5 towels
2 sofa doilies
Right sofa cushion cover
Left sofa cushion cover
Armchair Afghan
2 armchair doilies
Sofa slipcover
Assorted pictures, knick knacks (on shelves) and starburst
clock on R. and U. walls

BEDROOM (offstage preset)

Large beach towel
Folded newspaper
Spiral notebook (small)
Pen
Crush proof box cigarettes
Black Bic lighter
6 loose bullets (old)
6 boxed bullets (new)
Wrist watch (Jessie's)
Cardboard star kist tuna box:
1 old calculator

Small brown bag w/red ribbon inside
Manilla legal envelope w/Dawson written on face
Square piece of paper w/Cecil's phone number clipped to
manilla envelope
Assorted size boxes gift wrapped w/assorted types of gift
paper

ATTIC

Old shoebox (no label):
Gun wrapped in sheepskin
Old package of pipe cleaners
Gun oil
Cleaning cloth
Home made hanger cleaning rod w/cloth inserted

COSTUME PLOT

THELMA

White half-slip
Red & white house dress
Light blue embroidered sweater
Tan tights (Capezio hold 'n stretch—long suntan)
Glitzy house slippers

JESSIE

Grey floral blouse
Grey courduroy pants
Grey belt
Black sweater
Black socks
"top-sider" type shoes

AUTHOR'S NOTE ON REVISIONS

In light of the Broadway production in 2004, and the passing of two decades in the play's life, I would like to update the following lines so that the play feels contemporary. If you decide to do the play as a historical piece, you can, of course, use the old words in these places. The only thing I ask is that you not mix and match, i.e., use either the old text or the new text below, not both.

Page	Revised Text
10	JESSIE. Maybe an old blanket or towels we got at a flea market sometime?
17	JESSIE. You got me that nice powder, Loretta got me a new robe, pink probably, and ...
20	JESSIE. And they won't deliver for less than twenty-five dollars' worth. What I do is tell them what we need and tell them to add on batteries until it gets to twenty-five dollars.
20	MAMA. ... that he's getting married, or how about he's cut his hair, wouldn't that be nice?
23	JESSIE. Oh, everything from you and me to North Korea. MAMA I think we can leave the Koreans out of this.
36	JESSIE. ... if I wanted to, but you were going to watch *Kojak*. What did he ...
36	JESSIE. Now, you know Schmidts delivers on Wednesdays and Saturdays, and they leave the order blank in an egg box ...
45	MAMA. Let's take Loretta to the Fishnet and have those fried clams.
49	JESSIE. To Dawson and Loretta and the Koreans and epilepsy and ...
54	MAMA. I think I'll stay here. All they got is decaf.
55	JESSIE. I want Loretta to have my little clock radio.

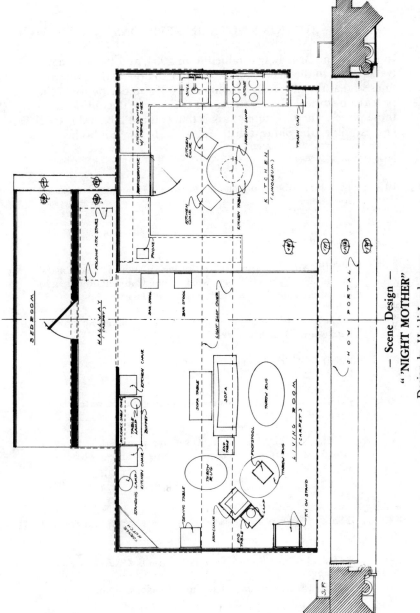

— Scene Design —
"NIGHT MOTHER"
Design by Heidi Landesman

NEW PLAYS

★ **BE AGGRESSIVE by Annie Weisman.** Vista Del Sol is paradise, sandy beaches, avocado-lined streets. But for seventeen-year-old cheerleader Laura, everything changes when her mother is killed in a car crash, and she embarks on a journey to the Spirit Institute of the South where she can learn "cheer" with Bible belt intensity. "...filled with lingual gymnastics...stylized rapid-fire dialogue..." *–Variety.* "...a new, exciting, and unique voice in the American theatre..." *–BackStage West.* [1M, 4W, extras] ISBN: 0-8222-1894-1

★ **FOUR by Christopher Shinn.** Four people struggle desperately to connect in this quiet, sophisticated, moving drama. "...smart, broken-hearted...Mr. Shinn has a precocious and forgiving sense of how power shifts in the game of sexual pursuit...He promises to be a playwright to reckon with..." *–NY Times.* "A voice emerges from an American place. It's got humor, sadness and a fresh and touching rhythm that tell of the loneliness and secrets of life...[a] poetic, haunting play." *–NY Post.* [3M, 1W] ISBN: 0-8222-1850-X

★ **WONDER OF THE WORLD by David Lindsay-Abaire.** A madcap picaresque involving Niagara Falls, a lonely tour-boat captain, a pair of bickering private detectives and a husband's dirty little secret. "Exceedingly whimsical and playfully wicked. Winning and genial. A top-drawer production." *–NY Times.* "Full frontal lunacy is on display. A most assuredly fresh and hilarious tragicomedy of marital discord run amok...absolutely hysterical..." *–Variety.* [3M, 4W (doubling)] ISBN: 0-8222-1863-1

★ **QED by Peter Parnell.** Nobel Prize-winning physicist and all-around genius Richard Feynman holds forth with captivating wit and wisdom in this fascinating biographical play that originally starred Alan Alda. "QED is a seductive mix of science, human affections, moral courage, and comic eccentricity. It reflects on, among other things, death, the absence of God, travel to an unexplored country, the pleasures of drumming, and the need to know and understand." *–NY Magazine.* "Its rhythms correspond to the way that people—even geniuses—approach and avoid highly emotional issues, and it portrays Feynman with affection and awe." *–The New Yorker.* [1M, 1W] ISBN: 0-8222-1924-7

★ **UNWRAP YOUR CANDY by Doug Wright.** Alternately chilling and hilarious, this deliciously macabre collection of four bedtime tales for adults is guaranteed to keep you awake for nights on end. "Engaging and intellectually satisfying...a treat to watch." *–NY Times.* "Fiendishly clever. Mordantly funny and chilling. Doug Wright teases, freezes and zaps us." *–Village Voice.* "Four bite-size plays that bite back." *–Variety.* [flexible casting] ISBN: 0-8222-1871-2

★ **FURTHER THAN THE FURTHEST THING by Zinnie Harris.** On a remote island in the middle of the Atlantic secrets are buried. When the outside world comes calling, the islanders find their world blown apart from the inside as well as beyond. "Harris winningly produces an intimate and poetic, as well as political, family saga." *–Independent (London).* "Harris' enthralling adventure of a play marks a departure from stale, well-furrowed theatrical terrain." *–Evening Standard (London).* [3M, 2W] ISBN: 0-8222-1874-7

★ **THE DESIGNATED MOURNER by Wallace Shawn.** The story of three people living in a country where what sort of books people like to read and how they choose to amuse themselves becomes both firmly personal and unexpectedly entangled with questions of survival. "This is a playwright who does not just tell you what it is like to be arrested at night by goons or to fall morally apart and become an aimless yet weirdly contented ghost yourself. He has the originality to make you feel it." *–Times (London).* "A fascinating play with beautiful passages of writing..." *–Variety.* [2M, 1W] ISBN· 0-8222-1848-8

DRAMATISTS PLAY SERVICE, INC.
440 Park Avenue South, New York, NY 10016 212-683-8960 Fax 212-213-1539
postmaster@dramatists.com www.dramatists.com

NEW PLAYS

★ **SHEL'S SHORTS by Shel Silverstein.** Lauded poet, songwriter and author of children's books, the incomparable Shel Silverstein's short plays are deeply infused with the same wicked sense of humor that made him famous. "...[a] childlike honesty and twisted sense of humor." –*Boston Herald*. "...terse dialogue and an absurdity laced with a tang of dread give [*Shel's Shorts*] more than a trace of Samuel Beckett's comic existentialism." –*Boston Phoenix*. [flexible casting] ISBN: 0-8222-1897-6

★ **AN ADULT EVENING OF SHEL SILVERSTEIN by Shel Silverstein.** Welcome to the darkly comic world of Shel Silverstein, a world where nothing is as it seems and where the most innocent conversation can turn menacing in an instant. These ten imaginative plays vary widely in content, but the style is unmistakable. "...[*An Adult Evening*] shows off Silverstein's virtuosic gift for wordplay...[and] sends the audience out...with a clear appreciation of human nature as perverse and laughable." –*NY Times*. [flexible casting] ISBN: 0-8222-1873-9

★ **WHERE'S MY MONEY? by John Patrick Shanley.** A caustic and sardonic vivisection of the institution of marriage, laced with the author's inimitable razor-sharp wit. "...Shanley's gift for acid-laced one-liners and emotionally tumescent exchanges is certainly potent..." –*Variety*. "...lively, smart, occasionally scary and rich in reverse wisdom." –*NY Times*. [3M, 3W] ISBN: 0-8222-1865-8

★ **A FEW STOUT INDIVIDUALS by John Guare.** A wonderfully screwy comedy-drama that figures Ulysses S. Grant in the throes of writing his memoirs, surrounded by a cast of fantastical characters, including the Emperor and Empress of Japan, the opera star Adelina Patti and Mark Twain. "Guare's smarts, passion and creativity skyrocket to awesome heights..." –*Star Ledger*. "...precisely the kind of good new play that you might call an everyday miracle...every minute of it is fresh and newly alive..." –*Village Voice*. [10M, 3W] ISBN: 0-8222-1907-7

★ **BREATH, BOOM by Kia Corthron.** A look at fourteen years in the life of Prix, a Bronx native, from her ruthless girl-gang leadership at sixteen through her coming to maturity at thirty. "...vivid world, believable and eye-opening, a place worthy of a dramatic visit, where no one would want to live but many have to." –*NY Times*. "...rich with humor, terse vernacular strength and gritty detail..." –*Variety*. [1M, 9W] ISBN: 0-8222-1849-6

★ **THE LATE HENRY MOSS by Sam Shepard.** Two antagonistic brothers, Ray and Earl, are brought together after their father, Henry Moss, is found dead in his seedy New Mexico home in this classic Shepard tale. "...His singular gift has been for building mysteries out of the ordinary ingredients of American family life..." –*NY Times*. "...rich moments ...Shepard finds gold." –*LA Times*. [7M, 1W] ISBN: 0-8222-1858-5

★ **THE CARPETBAGGER'S CHILDREN by Horton Foote.** One family's history spanning from the Civil War to WWII is recounted by three sisters in evocative, intertwining monologues. "...bittersweet music—[a] rhapsody of ambivalence...in its modest, garrulous way...theatrically daring." –*The New Yorker*. [3W] ISBN: 0-8222-1843-7

★ **THE NINA VARIATIONS by Steven Dietz.** In this funny, fierce and heartbreaking homage to *The Seagull*, Dietz puts Chekhov's star-crossed lovers in a room and doesn't let them out. "A perfect little jewel of a play..." –*Shepherdstown Chronicle*. "...a delightful revelation of a writer at play; and also an odd, haunting, moving theater piece of lingering beauty." –*Eastside Journal* (Seattle). [1M, 1W (flexible casting)] ISBN: 0-8222-1891-7

DRAMATISTS PLAY SERVICE, INC.
440 Park Avenue South, New York, NY 10016   212-683-8960   Fax 212-213-1539
postmaster@dramatists.com   www.dramatists.com